Positi...
For the Day

Banish Negative Thinking And Create
A Happier, Calmer, And Healthier You.

Harness The Power of Positive Thinking And
**Instantly Turn Every Day
Into A Great Day!**

A FeelFabToday Guide
by Rachel Robins

Positive Thoughts For The Day

All rights reserved.

Cover and internal images credited to:
© Nastia11 / ID 173263076 / photo's.com
© lapencia / Fotolia, © snyggg.de / Fotolia
© Colorlife /Fotolia, © GiZGRAPHICS / Fotolia
© baldyrgan /Depositphotos, © I.Petrovic /Depositphotos

ISBN-13: 978-1495320262

ISBN-10: 149532026X

Table of Contents

1

How This Book Can Help You Achieve Positive Thoughts Every Day

"I surround myself with things that make me happy. Why? Because... it makes me happy"

~ Kelly Epperson

Ever wonder how cheerful, upbeat people manage to seem so positive and calm about life? How do they get themselves into a happy place, and then manage to stay there? What habits have they developed that allow them so much positivity?

**When we pay attention to anything
we give it power. What power are you giving to
your current thought patterns?**

In this book we'll explore WHAT you really need to do to achieve daily positive thoughts, WHY these techniques are so important, and HOW to incorporate them effortlessly into your daily life.

Inside this book you'll discover:

- ♥ **What** steps you really need for daily positivity

- ♥ **Why** these methods are so empowering

- ♥ **How** to develop powerful, enriching daily habits

- ♥ **Successful** ways to banish negative thoughts

- ♥ **Easy** techniques to create a positive mindset

- ♥ **Simple** methods to turn your goals into a reality

- ♥ **Positive** thinking tips, quotes and affirmations

- ♥ **Instant** ways to feel happier, calmer and healthier

Our aim is to provide you with inspiration, ideas and encouragement for generating positive thoughts every day. We share with you the reasons why a positive mindset is so important for overall health and happiness. We'll help you focus on specific areas in your

2

life, and identify ways to create positive thoughts which, in turn, can lead to significant improvements for those areas.

When you break destructive thought patterns and develop empowering daily habits, you'll begin to feel the benefits immediately. It's our desire that when you follow the tips, techniques and methods in this book, you will be able to:

- **Banish** negative thoughts/overcome harmful beliefs

- **Develop** a set of powerful tools for daily positivity

- **Control** your thoughts and get what you want from life

- **Feel** happier, calmer and healthier whenever you want

As you build positive thought patterns, your levels of happiness, inner strength and health should all benefit, leaving you feeling ready to take on the world.

We hope you'll find the book inspiring and thought provoking…

2

WHAT Do You *Really* Need For Effortless Positive Thoughts?

*When we practice the art of positive thinking on a daily basis, we empower ourselves to lead a happier, calmer and healthier lifestyle. In this chapter we'll discover WHAT you **really** need to be doing (or not doing) to achieve a balanced and fulfilling life by utilizing positive daily thoughts.*

First, Identify What You Want

There are so many benefits to creating a healthy quota of positive thoughts every day. This can, however, mean different things to each person - therefore clearly understanding **what** you're trying to achieve is an important step in this process. You can then focus on **why** this is important to you, and **how** to set about achieving it.

For many people, it's about improving the quality of their life, and generally feeling more balanced and in control. For some, it's about identifying their priorities and ensuring they focus on them in a positive way. For others, it's about having a sense of purpose, in knowing that a positive approach will help them to achieve their goals in a faster and more proactive manner.

When we have a clear set of priorities, or a true sense of purpose, we are able to specifically focus our efforts in their direction. This level of focus means we can be more motivated and energized toward our objectives. We can put targeted goals and objectives in place, and quickly see the benefits of our actions.

"Purpose is the great divider that separates
those who are simply living,
from those who are truly alive."
~ Alex Rogers

The positive results from this approach means we can add massive benefits to our own lives, as well as that of our loved ones and those we care about.

Encouraging positive thoughts into our lives on a daily basis puts us in a strong position, whichever way they happen. When we are clear about the specific areas we would like to improve in our lives, then we can target our thoughts in those directions.

What areas in your life would you like to experience more achievement?

- ♥ More time with family and friends?

- ♥ Career progression or a complete change?

- ♥ Greater earning potential?

- ♥ Wellness and health goals?

- ♥ Personal development?

- ♥ Building on strengths or talents?

- ♥ Freedom to travel or be more independent?

- ♥ Religious or spiritual involvement?

- ♥ Development of hobbies or interests?

- ♥ Community involvement or being an influence for good causes?

- ♥ Future plans for family, lifestyle, etc?

Stop and think about what is really
important for YOU to achieve?

When we are able to understand our priorities we can ensure that our thoughts and actions are directed appropriately toward them. This means there is less opportunity for negative or unsupportive thoughts to creep in. If we do find ourselves drawn toward the negative, then it becomes much easier to allow positive thoughts to take over, once we have a clear set of goals.

"The purpose of life is to contribute in some way
to making things better."
~ Robert F. Kennedy

Do your current thoughts help to drive you closer to the things you want in life, or do your thoughts keep you stuck in a rut, at best, or at worst, drive you away from them?

Combat Negative Thinking

Too much negative thinking can be extremely destructive and may be a significant reason you struggle to achieve the goals you've set for yourself. Learning to overcome such restrictive thoughts and encouraging empowering positive thoughts into your life instead, is an important step toward achieving a happy, calm and healthy lifestyle.

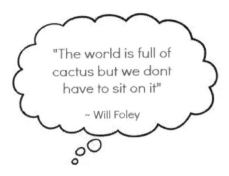

"The world is full of cactus but we dont have to sit on it"

~ Will Foley

If we constantly to listen to our own inner critic, or the 'internal voices' of others telling us we can't, won't, or shouldn't do something, then we are not likely to feel fulfilled. When we let others affect our self esteem, or when they encourage us to believe we are not good enough, it's vital to find strategies to overcome such destructive thoughts and feelings.

> *"The only place where your dream*
> *becomes impossible is*
> *in your own thinking."*
> *~ Robert H Schuller*

If we are too easily affected by negative external circumstances, are quick to blame others for our situation or are worried about being perfect all the time, then we will struggle to find balance and harmony.

The people we surround ourselves with can also cause us to think or feel negatively, if they themselves have a negative outlook on life, or are critical toward us or those we care about. People like this can sap your energy and leave you feeling down. Wherever possible avoid them, reduce any time spent with them, or find ways to tune them out and overwrite their negativity with your own happier thoughts.

"I will not let anyone walk through my mind
with their dirty feet."
~ Mahatma Gandhi

When we are able to build up resilience to life's challenges, form coping strategies, and add in a good dose of positive thinking to our daily routine, then we become much better equipped to take control of our own lives. We can therefore have a positive impact on our own life and the lives of those we care about.

"The difference between stumbling blocks and
stepping stones is how you use them."
~ Unknown

Unfortunately, we all have to face periods in our life when we are exposed to stress, hardship or various personal difficulties. However, the way in which we respond to these challenges can seriously affect our mental and physical well-being.

In a later chapter we'll go on to explore WHY we should strive to overcome negative thinking patterns and how to put in place empowering coping strategies.

When you have a strong level of self knowledge and are able to be positively in control of your thoughts, you are in a great position to enjoy the rewards of your achievements and to feel happy and fulfilled.

Converting negative self talk into positive empowering self talk can be an ongoing challenge. However it is well worth the journey - adding daily positive thoughts to your armory is one of the key tools to achieving a calmer, healthier and more fulfilled life.

"We cannot direct the wind
but we can adjust the sails."
~ Author Unknown

Understand The Power Of Words

Words are so much more powerful than most of us realize. On the surface, they help us communicate. For example when we express our emotions, impart information, raise alarms, are feeling motivational or destructive, and when we educate or demonstrate ideas.

With words, we can influence how others feel and the outcome of various situations. We can also use them to the same effect with ourselves. They can be used to positively motivate and encourage, or they can be used to hurt and be destructive.

Areas where words can have a powerful effect:

- ◆ The words *other people* use **toward us**
- ◆ The words *other people* use **toward other groups or individuals**
- ◆ The words *we use* **toward other people**
- ◆ The words *we use* **toward ourselves**

When we are constantly exposed to negative, unhealthy, damaging, sad, unsupportive words it will have a corresponding negative impact on our mood and well-being. On a daily basis we may listen to the news on TV or radio, read the papers, argue with a family member, be nagged at by the boss, overhear someone complaining, and so on. All these negative words and emotions can build up and leave us feeling down.

"If you keep on saying things are going to be bad,
you have a good chance of becoming a prophet."
~Isaac Bashevis Singer

Compare that to times when you've read a motivational book, spent time laughing and having fun with your family, received a compliment, been encouraged by a friend on a new project, or been thanked for time you spent on a worthwhile cause. The positive words and feelings can directly affect the thoughts that go on inside your head, and therefore how you feel.

The words we hear, and use, have the power to impact us on both an emotional and physical level.

Have you ever taken the time to listen to the words you are exposed to every day? Do they sound like:

- Encouragement or discouragement?
- Satisfaction or dissatisfaction?
- Gratitude or resentment?
- Healthy or unhealthy?
- Uplifting or downtrodden?
- Smart or stupid?
- Knowledgeable or ignorant?
- Positive or negative?
- Successful or defeatist?
- Supportive or hurtful?

"But if thought corrupts language,
language can also corrupt thought."
~ George Orwell, 1984

Are you aware of the language you personally use?

When you speak to others and to yourself do you generally use the same types of words, or do you change the words you select?

Some people are very good at being supportive toward others, but are hard and unforgiving when it comes to themselves. Others may carry around a strong sense of self belief ,and yet use negative language toward other people by being argumentative, stubborn, critical and hard to please, or just plain difficult.

 Take some time out to analyze the way you communicate to both others and to yourself

Monitor yourself over a period of a few days and note the words you use. Also, note the responses you receive from others and how you feel as a result of your self-talk.

Take note of the following:

♦ When you speak to others is it mainly with a positive or negative tone?

♦ How do people react when you use negative, harsh language?

♦ How do people react when you use supportive, encouraging language?

♦ How to you feel after you've communicated in either of these ways?

♦ When you speak to yourself is the language mainly positive or negative?

♦ Do you have any habitual words you use toward yourself?

♦ Does any of your self talk demonstrate self doubt or low self worth?

When you take time out to study the words you use and your habitual communication style, you may surprise yourself. Are there ways you could improve and have a greater impact?

By practicing daily positive thoughts we are able to shift our focus toward the use of empowering words. By becoming aware of the impact our words can have, we are able to take control of our language and therefore steer ourselves in a better direction.

"There is music in words, and it can be heard
you know, by thinking."
~ E.L.Doctorow

Take the time and effort to think about (and plan) your daily words. In a later chapter we'll look at how to create a successful plan for using empowering words on a daily basis.

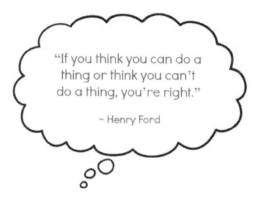

"If you think you can do a thing or think you can't do a thing, you're right."

~ Henry Ford

In the meantime, have a think about how often you use words in the example list below and how often you could add such words in to your daily thoughts?

Accomplishment	Achievement
Action	Adventure
Amazing	Angelic
Appealing	Attractive
Awesome	Beautiful
Believe	Brave
Brilliant	Calm
Celebrate	Certain
Courageous	Creative
Effective	Effervescent
Encouraging	Energized
Engaging	Enthusiastic
Excellent	Exciting
Fabulous	Fantastic
Fortunate	Free
Fun	Genuine
Giving	Great
Growing	Happy
Healing	Healthy
Heavenly	Idea
Imaginative	Innovative

Joy	Kindness
Knowledge	Light
Lively	Marvelous
Masterful	Motivating
Nurturing	Open
Optimistic	Plentiful
Positive	Powerful
Productive	Progress
Rejoice	Rewarding
Respectful	Smile
Spirited	Spiritual
Success	Superb
Supportive	Surprising
Terrific	Thrilling
Transforming	Up
Valuable	Vibrant
Welcome	Well
Wholesome	Willing
Wonderful	Worthy
Wow	Yes

Show Compassion Toward Yourself

Adopting positive thought processes means we are providing ourselves with a higher level of self-care.

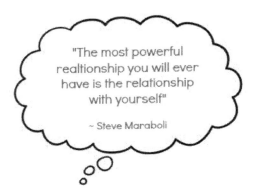

"The most powerful realtionship you will ever have is the relationship with yourself"

~ Steve Maraboli

When we treat ourselves respectfully and place a high value on our own welfare, we should feel the benefits in both our emotional and physical well-being. This, in turn, benefits those around us, and can increase our sense of enjoyment in life.

It is often too easy to become sidetracked with life's problems, and to let them overwhelm us. From time to time, we all make mistakes, behave inappropriately, become self obsessed, forget important things, feel down and lose focus.

*"A car can't operate without the mechanical systems
working, but it can operate with a few
dents and scratches...,
you are the same."*
~ Mike Dolan

However, when these challenges arise we should
show kindness toward ourselves and seek solutions, not
blame.

You wouldn't say to a friend:

- You'll never be able to start your own business
- You won't find a new partner who respects you
- It's pointless trying to learn new things now
- Don't try because you'll fail
- You're stupid
- You're not worthy of the effort

Instead, you'd be more likely to show
encouragement, support, or compassion for their
frustrations. The same should apply to the care we
show for ourselves. If you hear yourself using these
types of words immediately find alternative ways to **re-
position your response** toward life's challenges and
set-backs.

"When we give ourselves compassion, we are opening our hearts in a way that can transform our lives."
~ Kristin Neff

A balanced response, without self pity is far healthier than dwelling on any negatives. Whilst it may only be natural to initially feel disappointed, frustrated, upset or annoyed when bad things occur, too much emphasis on these issues will hamper your ability to move forward. However, when you learn how to put things into perspective, not blaming yourself and instead, take control of a situation, you can keep moving forward in a positive manner.

We can always learn from our mistakes, and try again tomorrow. By accepting our flaws, not trying to be perfect, and letting our inner selves go, we can increase our resilience to life's challenges.

"And now that you don't have to be perfect, you can be good."
~ John Steinbeck

 When we are in control of our thoughts and emotions we in a powerful position to feel confident, happy and secure

Break Bad Habits

Most of us will have developed some form of habitual self-talk that holds us back and prevents us from achieving what we desire.

Negative thinking, especially the negative thoughts we repeat to ourselves over and over, can be highly detrimental to our well-being. Such thoughts breed fear and anxiety, stop us from moving forward and lower our self esteem. Destructive thoughts and feelings can take the form of guilt, blame, anger, shame, disappointment, worry, fear, sadness and so on. None of these feelings are helpful, especially when experienced over a long period of time, and can also be detrimental to our physical health.

"Holding on to negative feelings and past circumstances is like placing a lock on your soul."
~ Charles F. Glassman

Many of these emotions are developed over a lifetime, and can be hard to shake. Learning to recognize and then break destructive thinking patterns can be difficult, but the effort is definitely worthwhile.

Every thought is a seed.
If you plant crab apples,
don't count on harvesting
Golden Delicious.

~Bill Meyer

Later on we'll look at ways of tuning in to your thought processes, how to interpret external events, and your choices for how they affect you.

Can you spot any of your unhelpful thinking habits?

- Blaming yourself for someone else's bad behavior?

- Fuming over an argument and not letting go?

- Obsessing over small things that you know aren't important?

- Getting angry over events you have no control over (weather, traffic, rude people, etc)?

- Feeling guilty about past events?

- Dwelling on your perceived inadequacies?

- Worrying about events that may never happen?

◆ Holding back for fear of failure?

◆ Expecting the worst to happen?

When we use empowering positive thoughts on a daily basis, we can begin to reverse our bad habits, and replace them with powerful positive ones instead.

"The best way to break a bad habit is to drop it."
~Leo Aikman

Recognize and Acknowledge The Good

Everyone has a mixture of good and bad things in their life. Unfortunately, it can be easy to become distracted by the problems and challenges we face, and forget to take account of the positive areas in our life.

Rather than focus on what you do not have, or any issues you're dealing with, take time out to list all the positive things you have in your life at the moment.

Positive areas to consider:

♥ People you care about or who care about you (and what makes them so special)

♥ Your health and well-being

♥ Financial security or income you receive

- ♥ Community or groups you are involved with

- ♥ Your home, warmth, food, clothing, possessions

- ♥ Access to information or education

- ♥ Skills or talents you possess

- ♥ Opportunities for personal development

- ♥ Time available to spend on things you enjoy or with those you care about

- ♥ Bad things that can happen, which you are fortunate enough not to have experienced

- ♥ Freedom to laugh and express yourself

- ♥ Support others have given to you along the way

*"A happy person is not a person in a certain set
of circumstances, but rather
a person with a certain set of attitudes."
~Hugh Downs*

It's sometime easy to take for granted the things we have in our lives that are actually really important to us.

By recognizing their value and regularly acknowledging their existence, we are adding to our quota of *daily positive thoughts*.

"If you count all your assets, you always show a profit."
~ Robert Quillen

A healthy appreciation of the good in our lives will never cause us a problem. However, forgetting to regularly acknowledge and cherish these wonderful things is a badly missed opportunity.

Reprogram Your Subconscious

If we are able to re-program our subconscious to receive greater levels of positive information then it becomes easier for us to feel optimistic and hopeful. We are then in a much stronger position to focus on achieving what we desire, and allowing positive thoughts to permeate our mind every day.

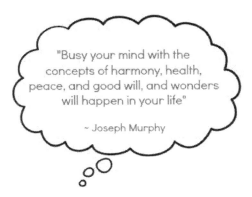

It's no secret that we are heavily influenced by our environment from an early age. The messages we receive from those we are close to and the world at large help to shape our way of thinking. We are influenced in a huge variety of ways; for example, by the words, actions and beliefs of those around us, both directly and indirectly.

"Only one thing registers on the subconscious mind:
repetitive application - practice.
What you practice is what you manifest."
~ Fay Weldon

We are all born with character traits inherent to us as individuals. However, some of the ways we think as adults are learned responses. These have been developed subconsciously over many years.

Examples of things we subconsciously respond to:

- Money and financial status
- Fear of failure or rejection
- Response to conflict or arguments
- Eating habits
- Desire to please others
- Beauty or perceived beauty
- Need to travel or keep moving

- Commitment
- Acts of kindness
- Good or bad news

People who received positive, enthusiastic, supportive messages early on in their lives are more likely to have a higher level of self confidence and self esteem. Those who were surrounded by negativity or lacked support when growing up may struggle with negative internal messages, often at a subconscious level. Unfortunately, we are also surrounded by much negativity in the media and the world in general.

All too often we are quick to think about what we don't want/have, as opposed to want we do want/have. This reiterates the wrong messages to our subconscious.

Examples such as:

- I don't have enough money **versus** I need to find a way to generate more income

- I'm not smart enough **versus** I don't know enough about that subject yet, so I'll invest in some training to broaden my knowledge

- Bad things always happen to me **versus** my run of bad luck is behind me, only good things will happen from now on

- I hate this neighborhood **versus** I'm adding 'move house' to my list of goals and will make a list of action points to get things started

- If I change jobs I might not like the people there **versus** the change will be good for me and I could make some new friends as well

By stating your desires in a positive light, you are telling your subconscious mind that that is the way you want it to process messages.

> *"Whatever we plant in our subconscious mind*
> *and nourish with repetition and emotion*
> *will one day become a reality."*
> *~ Earl Nightingale*

Recognizing your own responses to negative messages, along with consciously processing the daily bombardment of information we are now exposed to, is not a simple task. However, when you make a conscious effort to ensure you are receiving and reinforcing greater levels of positive, as opposed to negative messages, then you will help to minimize any self-limiting beliefs.

When you provide your subconscious with supportive & positive information it will help to steer you towards your goals, and increase your sense of wellbeing

Surround yourself with positive people, who want to see you do well and who will celebrate your successes in life, and you'll benefit from their enthusiasm and optimism.

"Surrounded by people who love life, you love it too; surrounded by people who don't, you don't."
~ Mignon McLaughlin

When you learn to think about things in a positive way, and regularly reinforce these 'feel good' messages, then positive thoughts become a natural part of your daily habits and will pop to the surface subconsciously.

Attract The Good Stuff - Believe and Achieve

Effortlessly achieving positive thoughts every day is made so much easier when you eliminate or minimize the time wasting and energy sapping activities or influences in your life. When you focus on productive activities, surround yourself with positive people or situations, and measure your achievements, you will begin to see more and more good things happening.

"If you can dream it, then you can achieve it.
You will get all you want in life if you
help enough other people get what they want."
~ Zig Ziglar

By following certain steps, it is possible to attract into our lives the things that make us feel satisfied, content and fulfilled. Later in the book we'll look at how to achieve these steps to continually attract more of the good things into our lives. For some people, this may take the form of material possessions and wealth building, whereas others may desire greater levels of friendship, religion, spirituality, love and well-being.

When we experience high levels of positive emotions we also appear to other people as someone who feels good to be around. We benefit from greater levels of social contact plus opportunities to bring new and exciting things into our lives. By being open to new experiences and projecting a positive outlook, you are in a great position to attract more of the things you want from life.

"Whatever the mind can conceive and believe,
it can achieve."
~ Napoleon Hill, Think and Grow Rich

It helps to be clear in your own mind as to what you really want, and whether these things will make you feel happy and fulfilled. Writing down your desires can allow you to visualize what it is that you **really** want, so you can then explore how to go about attracting these things.

What large and small things would you like to bring into your life?

- More wealth or financial security?

- Supportive, caring relationships with family?

- New friends?

- Different career or business start up?

- Opportunities to get out and try new experiences

- Develop a skill and share your interest with others

- Health and wellness?

- Better diet or personal fitness?

- Change your appearance?

- Opportunities to learn or study?

- Move to a new city or country?

- Change your home environment?

> Attracting more of what you want often comes
> down to simply being clear about your specific
> desires, & taking relevant action
> to bring them closer to you

In the same way that when you make a point to look out for yellow cars, you begin to see yellow cars everywhere, you will begin to see opportunities develop in the areas that matter most to you.

When you reduce the time you spend thinking about negative stuff, worrying, or stressing about things that won't matter in the long run, then you are less mentally exhausted and able to focus on the positive. By not over thinking and keeping your thoughts simple and focused on your desires, then you have positioned yourself accordingly to keep attracting good things into your life.

Much has been written about the Law of Attraction, which focuses on how to attract abundance into our lives by following certain laws of the Universe. These types of discussions are beyond the scope of this book, however, there are many books written on the subject of the Law Of Attraction, which may be worth exploring further, if you're interested in this subject.

People who are of an optimistic nature, and who regularly practice the art of positive thinking are much more likely to be happier, calmer and healthier than those who have a negative outlook on life. Having a positive focus, practicing daily positive thoughts and believing in yourself means you're positioning yourself to achieve great things.

"Happiness is an attitude.
We either make ourselves miserable, or happy and
strong. The amount of work is the same."
~ Francesca Reigler

3

WHY You Should Practice Positive Thoughts Every Day

In this chapter we'll explore WHY practicing positive thoughts every day is so powerful. We'll discover why we spend so much time on negative thoughts and how to change this mindset. We'll also look at ways these new thought patterns can benefit you, how they can help you get what you want, and can lead to a happier, calmer, healthier you.

<u>Why Wouldn't You?</u>

There are so many benefits to having a positive outlook as opposed to a negative one. When we feel good, we're capable of achieving so much more than when we feel down. Obviously, it's not possible to feel great all the time, or to constantly have positive thoughts. However, tipping the scales in your favor is well worth the effort. Working toward a healthy balance of good thoughts, with a positive overall approach means you've strengthened many aspects of your life, and that of those around you.

When we are optimistic and feel good, we are able to be more productive, energized, motivated, enthusiastic and fun to be around.

It isn't our position but our disposition which makes us happy.

~Author Unknown

How many positive emotions can you think of?

♥ Excitement

♥ Anticipation

♥ Joy

♥ Gratitude

♥ Love

♥ Comfort

♥ Contentment

♥ Amusement

♥ Lighthearted

♥ Kindness

♥ Pride

♥ Assertive

♥ Resilient

♥ Hopeful

Too many negative emotions mean we are less able to cope with life's difficulties, and may find ourselves stuck or unable to move forward. When you practice daily positive thoughts, you are strengthening your ability to tackle adversity and obstacles, meaning you will find it much easier to achieve a healthy, happy balance in your life.

> *"Things turn out best for the people*
> *who make the best out of the*
> *way things turn out."*
> *~Art Linkletter*

The Negative Programming Factor

It's only natural to be inclined toward negative thinking. Our brains were programmed very early on during human development to help prepare us for the dangers we could face every day. Our survival instinct meant we needed to be constantly alert to potential dangers, and therefore focus on avoiding and escaping dangerous situations.

The type of dangers our ancestors faced are not so relevant in our modern lives; however, the instincts are still there. This means that we need to pro-actively focus on positive emotions, and to overcome the urge to let negativity take control.

> *"The mind is its own place, and in itself*
> *can make a Heaven of Hell, a Hell of Heaven."*
> *~ John Milton*

By making a conscious effort to regularly use a set of powerful techniques that reinforce a positive attitude, you can re-train your brain to make lasting change for the better. Understanding this issue, and then taking control of your thoughts means you can reverse many of your self limiting beliefs over time.

What thoughts currently hold you back?

- I can't do that
- I don't have any valuable talents
- I'm no good with money
- I should be more extroverted
- I'm not a good communicator

- I don't have what it takes to start a business
- I'll never be smart at anything
- I'm too old to start a new career
- I'm not intelligent enough to pass that exam
- People won't want me joining their group

Recognizing and understanding self limiting beliefs is the start of re-programming your thoughts toward the positive.

*"You have to expect things of yourself
before you can do them. "
~Michael Jordan*

When you feed the negative beliefs
you have towards yourself, or the world
in general, you give them power

Take away their power by replacing them with positive alternatives, and take charge of your future.

Changing your mindset

There are so many wonderful benefits to having a positive mindset.

When you put your energies into:

♥ Believing good things will happen

♥ Knowing you are capable of achieving many great things

♥ Being thankful for the good things you already have in your life

♥ Demonstrating optimism

♥ Comfortably tackling adversities as they arise

♥ Taking control of your thoughts

♥ Taking action toward your goals

...then you will benefit immensely.

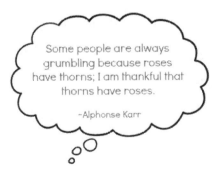

People will enjoy spending time with you, and will seek you out as a motivating and fun person to be with. You'll enjoy being in your own head so much more, and

should find that even when you experience moments of feeling blue, you can bounce back much more quickly.

Achieving a healthy balance of emotions, tipped toward the positive, has a load of health benefits too. People who are optimistic and regularly practice positive thinking are known to enjoy higher levels of wellness (both physical and emotional), decreased illness symptoms, and experience greater life expectancy rates.

Barbara L. Fredrickson, a Professor of Psychology at the University of North Carolina, and an expert in positive psychology, has made numerous studies into the effects of positive thinking.

Among other findings, she notes that those who practice positive thoughts are generally open to more possibilities, develop new skills, experience better moods, sustain the 'feel good' factor for longer periods and hold depressive symptoms at bay. Feeling good in the short term, when experienced regularly, can result in lasting positive change in our lives.

> *"Life is like a tree and its root is consciousness.*
> *Therefore, once we tend the root,*
> *the tree as a whole will be healthy."*
> *~Deepak Chopra*

Such change can have a positive impact in many areas of our lives such as improvements to our relationships, our work, our education and training, our hobbies and interests, our home life, our general well-being and health. We are better able to cope in the face of adversity and can recover faster from illnesses or set backs.

> When we withdraw the fuel for our negative beliefs, and instead focus on fuelling supportive self beliefs then we nurture a positive mindset.

Obviously, it's not as simple as just switching off the negative thoughts; however, we will look at ways to achieve this in the next chapter on 'Steps to Achieve'.

Our Thoughts Guide Our Actions

It is possible to learn how to control our thoughts as opposed to allowing our thoughts to control us. By taking charge and of what and how we think, we can then influence our feelings and behavior, and, therefore, our actions.

Positive thoughts = Positive actions

When we understand our own patterns of thinking, and guide them toward the positive, we can have a huge impact on our well-being, plus help to create stronger relationships with others. By recognizing our emotional responses to every day issues or even serious problems, along with the habitual thoughts that naturally follow, we can help to steer them in a better direction.

"If you don't like something change it; if you can't change it, change the way you think about it."
~Mary Engelbreit

When we become skilled at managing our emotional responses, and are able to ensure we don't get lost in negativity, we then place ourselves in a strong position. By ensuring that positive influences and thoughts guide us, we will then empower ourselves to take solution based action, moving us forward in a better direction.

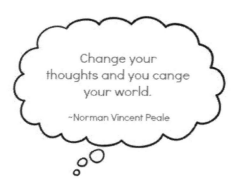

Change your thoughts and you cange your world.

~Norman Vincent Peale

If you focus on negative thoughts, you can get stuck in a destructive place and therefore struggle to take steps to improve any issues you're dealing with. If you can replace some of those thoughts with positive, solution oriented, uplifting thoughts then you will more likely to take relevant steps to help move you onward.

Build Inner Strength

One of the great ways to build inner strength is to point your daily thoughts toward recognition of your own personal qualities, by forgiving your shortcomings, and by accepting and appreciating yourself for who you are.

Having strong inner beliefs and values can benefit you in many ways. For example, developing the confidence to start new things, achieving greater outcomes, building stronger relationships, and feeling more inspired.

When you experience negative emotions, this can lower your energy and enthusiasm for life, whereas when you build on your inner strengths, you find the capacity to overcome issues and forge forward.

"You have power over your mind - not outside events.
Realize this, and you will find strength."
~ Marcus Aurelius

Recognize and celebrate your natural strengths, and seek ways to enhance them further. Take time out to develop skills and activities you enjoy, and which fortify you. Don't waste time focusing on what you are not good at or are not fulfilled by.

Thinking empowering thoughts and feeling
positive about yourself is a great way to
build internal strength

A robust inner attitude means you are capable of facing and overcoming many obstacles or challenges. Practicing daily positive thoughts can be a great way to add to your mental resource, giving you the skills to help confront problems as they occur. Make them part of your daily habits and they will help you develop great inner strength throughout your lifetime.

"If you can change your mind,
you can change your life."
~ William James

Path To Personal Growth

Developing the habit of daily positive thoughts means we are also able to steer ourselves in the direction of personal growth and development. There are many ways to approach self improvement; many of these can help support your goals or you may find fulfilling in their own right.

Steps taken toward self improvement can have wide ranging benefits, both for yourself and for those around you.

Benefits of self improvement:

- ♥ Increase inner strength
- ♥ Develop new skills
- ♥ Utilize natural talents
- ♥ Improve self awareness
- ♥ Develop confidence
- ♥ Improve self esteem
- ♥ Growth of knowledge
- ♥ Provide new career opportunities
- ♥ Enhance personal relationships
- ♥ Improve emotional and physical health
- ♥ Increase happiness levels

Our thoughts and actions are a large factor in how much we get out of life. Therefore, focusing our attention daily on ways to achieve personal growth should be high on our agenda.

> *"Life is a gift, and it offers us the privilege, opportunity, and responsibility to give something back by becoming more."*
> *~ Tony Robbins*

Following a path for personal growth and development should be an ongoing process. It can be become a major part of your life, such as attending university or working specifically on areas to build confidence and self belief.

Or, it can be achieved with small daily actions, such as starting the day with positive affirmations or clearly stating your intentions for positive achievements.

Even small daily acts of positivity can propel you forward, help you to discover new paths, and enhance your life in ways you may not expect.

> *"The man who removes a mountain*
> *begins by carrying away*
> *small stones."*
> *~ Chinese Proverbs*

Getting What You Want

One of the main reasons for practicing positive thoughts is to enable you to focus on, and then get what you want. Your brain is far more powerful than you realize, so when you regularly direct your energies toward the things you want in life, positive results will naturally follow.

Correctly apply the power of positive thought and you will in turn affect many areas of your life.

What areas of your life would you life to have a positive influence on?

♥   Career

♥   Wealth building

♥   Romantic relationship

♥   Friendships

♥   Family relationships

♥   Quality time spent with loved ones

♥   Fitness or weight loss

♥   Health and wellness

♥   Stress levels

- ♥ Free time and fun activities
- ♥ Interests and hobbies
- ♥ Sporting achievements
- ♥ Holidays or travel

When we learn to focus our mind in the right way, our subconscious helps to identify new opportunities and to point us in their direction. Shifting negative thoughts and replacing them with positive ones is an important step in this process.

"A pessimist is one who makes difficulties of his opportunities and an optimist is one who makes opportunities of his difficulties."
~Harry Truman

Continually focusing, dwelling and worrying about the things we don't want in our life means that they play a greater part in our reality than they need to. They can become all consuming and have a detrimental effect on all areas of our life.

How much time each day do you currently spend positively concentrating on the areas of your life you would like to improve or change?

When you fill your mind with positive thoughts and create positive thinking patterns, then you will bring more of the things you care about into your world.

 Even small changes to your thought processes & focus can make a huge difference to your lifestyle & happiness levels

"The key to success is to focus our conscious mind on things we desire not things we fear."
~ Brian Tracy

Happier, Calmer and Healthier You

By harnessing the power of positive thinking you are making a significant commitment to your health. Having a plan for daily positive thoughts can be a part of this commitment.

There have been many studies into the health effects of positive thinking - according to the Mayo Clinic, people with an optimistic attitude may benefit from:

♥   Higher resilience to aliments
     (e.g. the common cold)

♥   Greater psychological well-being

♥   Less depression

49

- ♥ Better overall physical health
- ♥ Lower rates of disease from cardiovascular issues
- ♥ Less incidents of distress
- ♥ Greater ability to cope with stress
- ♥ Longer life expectancy

It's well known that negative emotions such as anxiety, depression, fear, worry and ongoing stress can suppress your ability to be physically and emotionally fit, to be successful in many areas of your life, or to move forward. On the flip side, experiencing positive emotions on a regular basis can drive creativity and enable you to take massive steps toward improving or changing your life.

Positive thoughts alone are not powerful –
the power source is the feelings & emotions
that they evoke, which in turn allow
you to become powerful

Establishing a habit of daily positive thoughts can be an essential part of enjoying a happy mindset, feeling calmer and more able to cope with life's difficulties.

"We become what we repeatedly do."
~ Sean Covey

By experiencing higher levels of positive emotions, driven by daily positive thoughts, you can also enjoy greater levels of general health and wellness.

Having a positive mindset reinforces the 'feel good' factor

However, after looking at the reasons WHY we should practice daily positive thoughts, the big question is HOW to successfully achieve them, and reap the benefits.

"Most folks are about as happy as they make up their minds to be."
~ Abraham Lincoln

4

Critical STEPS To Achieve Positive Thoughts Every day

In this chapter we'll identify HOW to achieve positive thoughts on a daily basis. We'll look at how to banish negative thinking, and how simple steps can build empowering thought patterns. Additionally we'll explore various techniques and methods you can employ to see consistently great results.

State What You Want

We've seen from the above chapters that practicing daily positive thoughts can be an extremely powerful tool in helping us to achieve what we want from life.

Being crystal clear on what you really value, and tying this in with a true sense of purpose, can help to guide the actions you then choose to take.

> *"If you don't go after what you want,*
> *you'll never have it.*
> *If you don't ask, the answer is always no.*
> *If you don't step forward,*

you're always in the same place."
~ Nora Roberts

By aligning our values, goals, and desires with our actions, behaviors, and the time spent on these acts, means we can feel happier and more satisfied with the direction our lives are heading. Empowering yourself by understanding the effects of daily positive thoughts allows you to move closer to achieving what you'd really like from life.

"Believe that you can run farther or faster.
Believe that you're young enough,
old enough, strong enough, and so on to
accomplish everything you want to do.
Don't let worn-out beliefs stop you from
moving beyond yourself."
~ John Bingham

Start by writing down any areas of improvements or changes you would like to make in your life:

♥ More time to spend on things that are enjoyable?

♥ Greater income?

♥ Career development or job changes?

♥ More varied social life?

♥ Time to focus on learning new skills?

- ♥ Explore new talents or follow your passions?

- ♥ Meet new people?

- ♥ Start or grow a business?

- ♥ Enhance personal relationships or find love?

- ♥ Be more tolerant

- ♥ Move house, city or country?

- ♥ Build confidence or self esteem?

- ♥ Tackle health issues?

- ♥ Manage stress in a healthy way?

- ♥ Be kinder?

- ♥ Banish negativity or self defeating behavior?

- ♥ Feel content and happy?

Identify the areas of your life you'd like to attract positive change to. You can then make it part of your daily focus for positive thoughts, followed by significant actions.

State your goals out loud. Be proud of them, commit to them. Work on them daily & start to see the changes happen

*Define what you want to improve,
change or achieve?*

State these goals out loud

*Create positive thoughts and affirmations
for your goals*

Say them out loud and commit to them 100%

Take meaningful actions toward the goals

*Notice opportunities as they arise and take
advantage of them*

Recognize and celebrate mini achievements

Reinforce with more positive thoughts

Reap the rewards

Pick a new goal

<u>Recognizing Negative Signals</u>

Everyone suffers from negativity from time to time, although their triggers, and the extent to which they remain in a negative state will differ.

A key step to improving daily positivity is to find ways to recognize and decrease negative thoughts and patterns.

Do you ever find yourself dwelling on things you have no control over, feeling grumpy for no significant reason, worrying about things or being hard on yourself?

Are there certain people, situations or times that create unpleasant thoughts which get trapped inside your head?

What triggers your negative thought patterns?

- Oversleeping
- Other people's bad moods
- Poor driving experience
- Being late
- Making a mistake
- Missing an event
- Losing something
- Bad weather

- Feeling unwell

- Worrying about 'what if…'

- Annoying daily events

- Things not working out as planned

- Feeling discontent

We all have negative patterns of thinking that we easily fall into. Try and recognize how you respond the various triggers. What are your initial reactions to these triggers? What emotions do you experience – irritation, anger, anxiety, stress, embarrassment, frustration?

Do you hear yourself saying things such as:

- I can't cope with the extra stress

- I'm so stupid for doing that

- My whole day is ruined now

- I can't be bothered

- It's too much pressure

- Nothing ever works out well

- It could only happen to me!

- Just my bad luck!

- Why me?

Are these catastrophic events that triggered these reactions? Or events such as sleeping through the alarm, getting stuck in traffic, being soaked in an unexpected downpour, not winning a contract after a presentation, or missing the start of a show?

It's easy and natural to focus on the negative stuff that happens. However if you can recognize your triggers, and how you respond to them, then you can put controls in place to swap negative thoughts for positive ones and get yourself re-focused. If you can catch the unpleasant thoughts early on, you can potentially stop them from forming or from taking over and unnecessarily controlling your moods.

Recognize your main triggers

Recognize your emotional responses

Listen to how you respond and notice the language you use

STOP *the thought pattern and* ***SWAP*** *for a proactive one*

Negative thoughts often have a way of creeping in, uninvited. However you can unlearn destructive patterns of thinking.

"I've tucked those negative thoughts in a drawer,
and for the most part,
though I know the drawer still exists,
it never gets opened."
~ K. Martin Beckner

When you actively increase your level of awareness, you will be able to recognize the signs early on, and take steps to counter any self-defeating thoughts, by replacing them with positive new patterns of thought behavior.

 What steps can you take today to change your negative thought patterns?

"Inspiration comes from within yourself.
One has to be positive.
When you're positive,
good things happen"
~ Deep Roy

<u>Managing and Replacing Negative Thoughts</u>

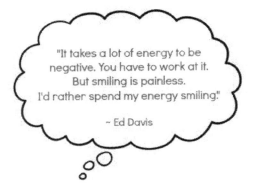

"It takes a lot of energy to be
negative. You have to work at it.
But smiling is painless.
I'd rather spend my energy smiling."

~ Ed Davis

Acknowledging and recognizing negative thought patterns is one thing, however it is our ability to control and replace them that is most important.

So how do we successfully challenge negative thought processes?

<u>STOP & SWAP!</u>

1. **Catch it early** – When a trigger occurs recognize it quickly and be ready to act.

2. **Use a STOP signal** to prevent the thought from escalating. Refuse to let it repeat or grow.

3. **Find a distraction** that can block the thoughts, especially if you can find something positive, funny or enjoyable to temporarily to break the cycle.

4. **Be constructive** – Shift your thoughts by reframing a situation. Interpret differently – change 'I was late for the meeting and now they'll all think I don't care' to 'Everyone knows I'm normally reliable, I'll explain the reasons later so there's no misunderstanding'.

5. **Review** – Congratulate yourself on taking control of your thoughts and actions. Once you're in a calmer, more positive frame of mind, check to see if there is   anything you can do to resolve outstanding issues, or to prevent a reoccurrence?

By taking positive action
it puts you back in control

When you catch yourself in a negative loop, being able to stop and re-direct your thoughts is critical. Over-thinking and dwelling on negative thoughts means we can get stuck in a loop of pessimism, unhappiness and discontentment. This, in turn, can impact on our ability to concentrate, be creative, find solutions, feel motivated, or move forward.

There are a number of tools you can use to STOP negative thoughts and put you in control:

♥ Visualize a large traffic STOP sign – hold that thought for 30 seconds

♥ Have a playlist of uplifting songs you can switch on and sing along to

♥ Imagine the unpleasant thought written down on a piece of paper. Now screw it up into a tight ball and throw it backwards over your shoulder.

♥ Use a rubber band to flick on your wrist as a reminder each time you start an unwanted thought

♥ Phone or meet up with a positive friend. Focus on anything other than problems. Re-visit the issue if necessary, only when you feel in control.

♥ Do something physical – go for a run, do the housework or walk the dog

♥ Imagine the thought and place it in a box. Tie the box up tightly with a big ribbon and place on a shelf for re-examination at a later date.

♥ Designate a specific time to concentrate on problems or challenges, when you can think them through calmly, and look for solutions. In the meantime, let them go, and get on with having a good day.

💜 Sleep on it. Things often look better in the morning.

Those who wish to sing, always find a song

~Swedish Proverb

Learning to **STOP** negative thoughts is part of the positive cycle. However, to be effective, you also need to **SWAP** any unpleasant thoughts for positive ones.

"It's snowing still," said Eeyore gloomily.
"So it is."
"And freezing."
"Is it?"
"Yes," said Eeyore. "However," he said, brightening up
a little, "we haven't had an earthquake lately."
~ A.A.Milne

Writing down any initial or regular negative head chatter can be a helpful way to see patterns you've developed, and to allow you to re-position these thoughts.

Try applying some of the following examples to your own life:

Negative Thought   *Positive Thought*

Negative Thought	Positive Thought
This project is too hard	I'll review the project from a different angle and ask for help if necessary
I'm not skilled enough	I'll find a way to improve my skills
I don't want management to change the team structure	The change could bring about benefits and opportunities for everyone
I don't know how - I'm bound to fail	I'll find someone to show me the ropes so I feel more confident
I overslept so now my day is ruined	I can make up the time and will pick up a better alarm clock at the store today
I can't afford it	It's important so I'll save up or work extra shifts
Aaaaaagggh!	Take a deep breath, relax, and take control...
Nothing ever works out	I'll change my approach and next time it will work
I'm worried that ...	Thank yourself for the concern, and be reassured that everything will work out OK
That presentation went really badly, I didn't do my best	Maybe the audience wasn't ready to buy yet. I can practice and improve for next time
It's too late to start now	Better late than never. Let's get going!

When you write it down, you can clearly see the negative thought patterns you experience. You can then see how easy to is to re-purpose these thoughts and how empowering this process is.

"Two people can have a middling day,
but one rounds up and the other rounds down."
~ Robert Brault

The formula allows you to take control, be flexible in your thinking and to choose which path you take going forward.

As you create new patterns of thinking you will notice a change in your emotions and feelings. It will become far easier to let go of debilitating feelings of fear, worry, shame, guilt or resentment and to replace them with feelings of hope, joy, gratitude, motivation, forgiveness and happiness.

Life's Not Perfect – Face Negatives Head On

Life isn't always a bed of roses and it's natural to feel negative from time to time. It's perfectly acceptable to have moments when life gets you down or you need to let off steam.

Ignoring, suppressing, and denying negative feelings can be detrimental to your long term welfare. However, over-thinking, dwelling and worrying too much can also be a major issue. Achieving an appropriate balance of negative and positive thoughts is the key.

> *"I've had a lot of worries in my life,*
> *most of which never happened"*
> *~ Mark Twain*

There are times when a negative situation or person arouses unpleasant emotions in us. It can be important, and healthy, to allow the thoughts and emotions to take form, providing they do not occur too often or are too detrimental. Having allowed the emotions to express themselves, you can then decide how to quickly move past them.

Face, Then Replace

Reasonable negative emotions should be given some space to breathe and to resolve themselves. The trick is not to allow them to linger for too long or to take over your life. That's when you need coping mechanisms or tools in your armory to fight them.

> *"There is little difference in people,*
> *but that little difference makes a big difference.*
> *The little difference is attitude.*
> *The big difference is whether it is positive or negative."*
> *~ W. Clement Stone*

If you find yourself getting stuck in a negative spot, but feel that you still need to tackle the prickly issue, try to park the problem and allow yourself to re-visit it at an allotted time later. Set aside a maximum time for reviewing your problem(s), and then have a fresh, fun task to move onto. Employ the various tactics discussed in this chapter to STOP and SWAP once your allotted time is up.

It's also worth recognizing that we need to be realistic about life's obstacles – there will always be challenges, hurdles and unexpected problems to overcome.

Allowing yourself time to consider any problems in a calm & proactive manner can be a great way to set yourself up for success later on

Negative thoughts are a natural way of coping with life's challenges, and we should embrace them, but not allow them to ever control us.

Gratitude and Thanks

There has been much research conducted into the benefits of demonstrating gratitude. Those who regularly express their gratitude are found to be healthier, more content and happier.

It is a natural human tendency to focus on the problems we encounter in life, to constantly be distracted with the things that go wrong and to dwell on things that upset or irritate us. Taking time out to focus instead on the positive things we have encountered can make a huge difference to our overall levels of satisfaction and happiness.

> *"Do not take anything for granted —*
> *not one smile or one person*
> *or one rainbow or one breath,*
> *or one night in your cozy bed."*
> *~Terri Guillemets*

By expressing gratitude and improving our outlook, we are also able to steer our thoughts toward achieving our goals. This in turn can help us to feel happier, calmer and healthier.

So how can you regularly demonstrate gratitude and express thanks to benefit from this habit?

♥ **Make it a daily habit** – Each night, when you to bed, list at least 3 things you are grateful for. Waking up and remembering these things is also a great way to start your day with positive thoughts.

♥ **Keep a journal** – Note down the all the things you are genuinely grateful for, including all the little things that normally go unnoticed.

♥ **Recognize the big** – There will important areas of your life such as health, loved ones, friendship, home, security, career, income and opportunities that may hold different value at different times in your life, and continue to change throughout your lifetime.

♥ **Recognize the small** – Note some of the happy incidents that occur each day such as receiving a compliment or a smile from a stranger, seeing a beautiful autumn landscape, the first spring flowers, enjoying a nice meal, no traffic holding you up, a sunny morning, your favorite tune playing on the radio and so on.

♥ **Notice how you feel** – What emotions do you experience as you go through your list? Satisfaction, joy, pride, happiness, love, contentment, humor, excitement or hope?

♥ **Link to your goals** – Be thankful for any achievements you make toward your goals, any opportunities that present themselves, plus any steps you make to move you closer to achieving what you want in life.

- **Personally thank someone** – Have you thanked others for their help, recognized their support, or acknowledged how important they are to you? If not, make a note to do so as soon as possible.

- **Remember to include yourself** – Acknowledge all the great things you've managed to achieve, proactive steps you've taken, and positive thoughts that replaced negative ones. Congratulate yourself! You're allowed to feel good about yourself!

- **Review and Maintain** – Look back at how well you've expressed your gratitude, think about how it makes you feel/the benefits you've gained (or could gain with more practice), and make a commitment to keep up this empowering habit.

These actions are not complicated, can be easy to do, and are extremely empowering. Developing a daily habit for stating your thanks and gratitude is a powerful way to achieve a positive mindset.

Thoughts and feelings of gratitude can also be shared with others, which may then help them to form empowering habits of gratitude. And you can take extra steps by being sure to openly recognize and thank others for their acts of support or kindness.

"Develop an attitude of gratitude, and give thanks for everything that happens to you, knowing that every step forward is a step toward achieving something bigger and better than your current situation."
~ Brian Tracy

Expressing our gratitude achieves more than just the 'feel good factor' – it can actually produce positive results. When we feel good, we act in a positive manner, are pleasant to be around and can make others feel good too. This can often open up more opportunities, and allows us to see the world in a better light.

72

Positive Affirmations For Daily Thoughts

"I am the greatest,
I said that even before I knew I was"
~ Muhammad Ali

Inspiration to include in our daily thoughts is all around us – the more we begin to notice things the more we'll keep seeing them. We are surrounded every day by things that are beautiful, funny, helpful, motivating, uplifting, – all of them can serve as fodder for our thoughts.

The question is, how do we start to notice them more, and allow our imagination to flow through into creating positive thoughts, and how do we put them to good effect?

A powerful way to achieve positive thoughts, with high impact, is to use positive affirmations

These are usually short statements, written in the present tense and personal to you. They can be extremely effective in helping you to focus on goals or areas of your life you want to improve upon, to tackle negative thinking, and to help guide your subconscious in a positive and empowering manner.

Affirmations can be broken down into categories, helping you to focus on the areas you would like to see the most improvements in.

Below are some examples of positive affirmations – what statements can you create for yourself?

Health and wellness

- ♥ I respect myself enough to take good care of my physical and emotional health

- ♥ I'm overcoming my illness as I know it's treatable

- ♥ I plan to live a long, happy, healthy and productive life

- ♥ I respect and care for my body with regular exercise and a good diet

- ♥ I take time out to relax and re-fuel my batteries

- ♥ I look forward to the future and live each day to the full

- ♥ I feel good about myself and my life

- ♥ I am the healthiest version of me I can be

- ♥ I am happy, calm and healthy

Personal development

- ♥ I accept that making mistakes is okay and I learn from their opportunities

- ♥ I know what I do today effects tomorrow and will make the right choices

- ♥ I have gained some great knowledge/experience and am doing the best I can with it so far

- ♥ I seek out opportunities to learn new skills and use my talents

- ♥ I commit to my goals and take action each day to move closer toward them

- ♥ I commit to actions that will make a difference

- ♥ I acknowledge my achievements and reward myself when appropriate

- ♥ I shall not stop, hesitate, or be distracted from achieving my dream

- ♥ I am motivated to do more, take action and enjoy the benefits

Confidence

- ♥ When I see my reflection I remember to stand tall, smile and look the world confidently in the eye

- ♥ When I think about myself, I see a strong, happy, healthy person

- ♥ I accept myself for who I am and I am proud to stand up for what I believe in

- ♥ I control my thoughts and choices so I feel good about myself

- ♥ I forgive myself for past behaviors, mistakes or poor choices

- ♥ I don't run from problems – I face them and seek solutions

- ♥ I have confidence in my abilities and trust myself to do the right thing

- ♥ I ignore my fears and face challenges head on

Lifestyle

- ♥ I take pleasure in the small, happy occurrences each and every day

- ♥ I notice beautiful things around me all the time

- ♥ I am thankful for the support of others and will reciprocate wherever possible

- ♥ I enjoy a good social life and commit to spend more time on activities I enjoy

- ♥ I surround myself with positive people who encourage and inspire me

- ♥ I treat others with respect, kindness and compassion

- ♥ I know that bad things happen but I will make the best out of the situation

♥ I enjoy sharing humor and fun activities with others

♥ I quickly replace negative thoughts with positive ones

♥ I find solutions to daily problems - I know that things work out okay in the end

♥ I don't get frustrated with things I cannot change

Our thought patterns can be quickly altered by using positive affirmations – they can help to alter the way you think and feel about yourself and the world around you.

Starting your day with a set of relevant & powerful statements is a great way to empower yourself, feel good & set the tone for a wonderful day

Building Blocks For Effortless Daily Positivity

Start your day with the intention
of having a great day.

There are many ways to achieve this. For example:

♥ Place positive quotes around your home or work

♥ Express gratitude

♥   State your intentions to carry out specific actions

♥   Positive affirmations

♥   Practicing mindful observations

Below are some of the building blocks for encouraging positive thoughts into your life on a daily basis:

1. **Accept and respect yourself for who you are** – Recognize your unique and special qualities, be proud to be you, and to live your life the way you want to.

2. **Notice all the positive things in your life** - Focus on the good things you have or that make you feel good, as opposed to the things you don't have or want, or cause you to feel negative. When you pay attention to the stuff you don't want in your life, you give it more energy. Instead, place your energies into focusing on all the positive things you have, the things you enjoy, and the people you care about.

3. **Express gratitude** – Be thankful for all the big and small blessings that surround you every day.

4. **Maintain positive relationships** – Relish the wonderful people you have in your life and the joy you can bring to each other. Don't allow problems to overwhelm or sabotage these relationships. Discuss the important stuff when necessary but ensure there's a healthy balance of fun, friendship and love involved.

5. **Plan for success** – Be clear on what you want and the steps you need to take to achieve your desires. You can then build these into your daily thoughts and habits, bringing them into reality much faster.

6. **Take time out** –Find some quite time each day when you can relax and clear your mind (even if it's only when you make a coffee or are stuck in traffic). You can unwind, de-stress, calmly assess your priorities, and check that your thought processes are supportive rather than detrimental.

7. **Let go** – You don't always need to be in control, or be all things to all people. Relax and take the pressure off; remember that if you're doing your best, then things will work out well in the end. Let go of resentments, anger, or harsh feelings toward others. Work toward dealing with these issues and moving past them. Forgive yourself if you've been

over critical in the past; be a good friend to yourself instead.

8. **Spend your precious time and energy intelligently** – Time and energy spent on negativity is wasted and you can never get it back. Minimize the time you allow yourself to discuss problems. Instead focus your energies on solution oriented thoughts, creativity, positive activities, uplifting people and moving toward your goals. If negative thoughts take over, use the STOP and SWAP technique.

9. **Take note of your feelings** – When you practice different techniques for increasing positivity, you'll become aware of how they effect your emotions. If you observe happy smiling children on the way to work, you make someone happy after complimenting them, achieve a milestone in your goals, truly express your gratitude for something or get lost in a happy thought, stop and note how you feel. Mini uplifts throughout your day can put you in a positive frame of mind, helping you to feel motivated and open to new experiences.

10. **Use language carefully** – The words we use can be incredibly powerful. Avoid *can't, won't, should have, if only, never again* style of words that are

linked to negative statements. Focus on what you can, will and are doing successfully. Recognize your strengths and qualities, celebrate your wins and believe in yourself. Your subconscious will absorb the positive language you use over time, and begin to make it part of your overall mindset.

11. **Recognize your power** – You have the power to control your thoughts and actions. Creating a positive mindset opens us up to more possibilities, means we're nicer to be around, enables us to help others, and allows us to enjoy greater levels of health.

Write It Down

Some people are very good at retaining lots of stuff in their head and creating thoughts as they need them. Others progress better when they write things down and/or see prompts when they need them.

Ideas for writing and how this can benefit you:

♥ **Gratitude journal** – Daily journal to jot down any good things that occur each day, your general thoughts on gratitude, or specific people/events you're thankful for. This can be a useful discipline to ensure you develop the process into an ongoing habit. It can also be motivating to look back at your notes, and may provide you with added inspiration at a later date.

♥ **Positivity scrapbook** – Build a collection of inspirational photos, magazine articles, pictures, quotes, notes to yourself, and so forth. This can help as a visual tool and thought stimulus for whenever you need a positivity boost.

♥ **STOP and SWAP notes** – Record your negative thoughts and practice replacing them with positively worded statements instead. Swap 'I never going to finish this project' to 'I've struggled but I'm going to ask for help/an extension/get training/approach from a new angle'. Seeing the options on paper, and repeating these mental exercises daily can be a great way to reinforce positive and proactive messages to your subconscious, turning this mindset into a natural positive daily habit.

♥ **Mini notebook** – Carry a small note pad around with you, so you can capture thoughts and ideas on the go. See something that inspires you? Capture it when it's fresh in your mind and then revisit it later so it's not forgotten.

♥ **Goals list** – When you write down the things you want to achieve and the steps you need to turn them into a reality, they become stronger. You can then track your progress, amend the goals each time you tick off your achievements, and focus your thoughts daily on taking steps to move closer to their completion.

♥ **Snapshots of Inspiration** – If there are specific quotes, sayings or personal mantras that inspire you, write them down and review them daily. These visual prompts can help keep you on track, remind you of your goals and keep them front of your mind.

♥ **Daily journal** – Writing down your thoughts, experiences, desires, etc, can be a great way of expressing yourself. Some people find it very cathartic to escape into the written word, plus, it can be a great way to look back at challenges you've overcome and your journey through life.

Writing things down it can be a helpful way to put your thoughts in order. These thoughts and ideas can be captured by hand or typed into a PC/laptop/phone. There are various tools you can use such as a printed diary/journal, printed forms, notebooks (spiral bound are good for removing pages if required) and smart phone apps. Dating your work is also a good idea, so you can look back at your progress.

> *"The art of writing is the art of*
> *discovering what you believe."*
> *~Gustave Flaubert*

The style, technique and frequency of writing can be as flexible as you want. Whatever style you choose, it can be a great way to capture changes and progress you make with your thought patterns. It allows you to listen to yourself, to observe your thought patterns (the bad and good), and to gain self knowledge.

Writing your thoughts down helps you practice the art of daily positive thinking.

Relaxation Techniques

Deep breathing and muscle relaxation can be used effectively to help achieve daily positive thoughts. It can sometimes be hard to actively think about what you want, are thankful for, are proud of, are aiming for, or to think through solutions.

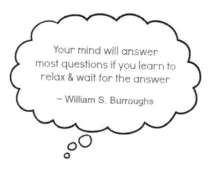

The noise of daily life can be filled with clutter, chaos and distracting thoughts.

Taking time out to mentally and physically relax can allow you to refocus on motivating and happy thoughts.

Relaxation techniques can be useful for unwinding, de-stressing, managing illnesses and generally quieting a busy mind.

If you can fit these exercises into your daily routines then they can also help increase your energy levels and boost your mood. It then becomes easier to organize your thoughts and ensure that positive thinking patterns prevail.

There are many forms of relaxation techniques and they generally have a combination of deep breathing with a progressive relaxation of the muscles.

Examples of relaxation techniques are:

♥   Relaxation breathing

♥   Progressive or passive muscle relaxation

♥   Massage, reflexology or reiki

♥   Prayer or meditation

♥   Tai chi or yoga

♥   Autogenics

♥   Light exercise such as walking, swimming, cycling or gardening

Many of these techniques can be self taught, although may be best learned initially through classes or one on one sessions conducted by a qualified practitioner.

Alternatively, you can create your own combination and style of relaxation. Find one that fits with your lifestyle, feels right for you, and allows you to interrupt chaotic thoughts and to re-focus your mind.

So how can you use relaxation methods to help achieve daily positive thoughts?

1.   Ideally, find a quiet place to sit or lay down.
2.   Make sure you feel comfortable.
3.   Close your eyes.

4. Focus on your breathing – concentrate on slowly breathing in/out in a regular rhythm, which will start to calm you down. Breathe in through your nose, and slowly out through your mouth.

5. Empty your mind of active thoughts. Visualize a blank piece of white paper or count backward slowly from 1000, picturing the numbers as you count.

6. Start to relax each muscle in turn – let go of any tension, start with your feet and work upward. Concentrate on relaxing each muscle at a time - foot, ankle, upper and lower leg, hips, abdomen and so on. Include your face, neck and scalp.

7. You should begin to feel your body become heavy and floppy at the same time.

8. Re-target certain areas if you're not completely relaxed.

9. Focus your thoughts toward something you find relaxing and enjoyable, such as walking around your garden, a park, painting or playing with your pet.

10. Banish any negative thoughts by mentally scrunching them into a ball and throwing them backward over your shoulder. Replace them with the relaxing thoughts above.

11. Once you're in control and fully relaxed focus on the positive thoughts you want to be having. This

could be expressing gratitude, visualizing yourself achieving your goals, personal affirmations, etc.

12. Smile and thank yourself for the relaxing time-out you've created.

Where possible, make specific times to practice these techniques regularly. Ideally, you'll be able to devote at least 20 minutes per day to an enriching relaxation method. However, if you struggle to find the time then even snatched moments on the train, in the bathroom, while boiling the kettle, waiting for the printer to warm up etc can be an opportunity to practice deep breathing and thought blocking exercises for a few minutes.

Regularly practicing relaxation techniques means you can quickly release tension in your body, clear your thoughts, and re-focus your mind in the positive direction you want it to go.

"Tension is who you think you should be.
Relaxation is who you are."
~Chinese Proverb

Laser Focus

When you're trying to ensure that you focus your mind toward empowering and positive thoughts each day, it can help to have some steps to follow and to refer to for the times when you become distracted.

"One reason so few of us achieve what we truly want is that we never direct our focus; we never concentrate our power. Most people dabble their way through life, never deciding to master anything in particular."
~ *Tony Robbins*

Throughout this book we've discussed the huge benefits that arise from daily positive thoughts. However, some of the techniques may require practice before they become a natural habit. Developing any new behavior patterns can take time and effort. To prevent yourself from slipping back into old patterns of thinking, you need to have some clear and simple processes to follow:

1. **Start with 1 thing** – Don't try to tackle everything all at once. If there is a major area of your life you want to improve, let this be your main focal point. For example if you want to improve your confidence in the workplace, then focus your thoughts in this direction. Use positive affirmations, visualization, set specific goals, STOP and SWAP any negative thoughts, and spend time finding solutions to your challenges. As your confidence grows, move on to a new area to set your sights on.

2. **Decide what works for you** – Use the techniques that resonate best with you. Do you respond well to inspirational quotes? Do you enjoy recording your thoughts in a journal? Do you benefit from writing down negative thoughts and re-wording them with positive statements instead? Do you find visualization works well after a relaxation break? Whatever works, do more of it. Keep it up, don't break the new habit. Focus on it hard until you start to feel the results.

3. **Choose your best time** – When are you at your most inspired or reflective? Maybe you would respond best to a set of inspiring messages at the start of the day, followed by a clear statement of your intentions for the day plus positive affirmations? Or perhaps ending the day with setting time aside to record your thoughts or to list the things you're grateful for?

4. **Be realistic** – Being positive all the time is not realistic. Life gets in the way and stuff happens. It can also be quite hard to create new patterns of thinking and develop new habits. Old ones creep back in uninvited. Don't worry if you find this happens – just take note and get back on track. Each time you re-engage with the art of positive thinking you will be benefiting yourself and those you care about in multiple ways.

5. **Congratulate and reward** – You've achieved some amazing things, even with small steps, when you spend time each day engaged in positive thoughts. Stop and reflect on how good it feels and praise yourself for a job well done. When you reach a positive milestone that you've set for yourself – smile, be happy and give yourself a reward.

 Use highly targeted thoughts throughout the day, & make sure to notice how you feel. Practicing empowering thoughts on a regular basis cannot fail to make you feel happier, calmer & healthier

Once you have practiced the various techniques for a reasonable period of time, you will develop natural positive thinking patterns without even realizing it. However, in the meantime **focus, focus, focus.**

"Every day is an opportunity to make
a new happy ending."
~Author Unknown

5

Concluding Thoughts

So why should you place so much importance on creating positive and empowering thoughts every day?

 Whatever we focus our attention on we give energy to

When you develop the habit of daily positive thoughts, you take a huge step toward achieving a happy and healthy balance in your life.

Focus on negative issues and you give them power over you. Instead focus on positive, pro-active, empowering thoughts, and they will absorb your energy and flourish.

The thoughts you focus on have a direct and meaningful impact on your life

From the moment you start your day, it's up to you to decide if it's going to be a good one. Although daily problems may arise, and things may not go as planned, there are always good moments that can be taken from every day. You can choose to have more positive experiences and emotions by thinking and acting in positive ways.

"You must start with a positive attitude
or you will surely end without one."
~Carrie Latet

Because we are only able to sustain one main thought at a time, then it may as well be a good one. You are ultimately in control of your thoughts, so do you choose to:

♥ Focus on negative thoughts that make you feel bad?

♥ Focus on empowering thoughts to make you feel good?

"Be miserable. Or motivate yourself.
Whatever has to be done,
it's always your choice."
~ Wayne Dyer

Throughout this book we've looked at WHAT, WHY and HOW to use daily positive thoughts to find personal strength and to help us feel happy, calm and healthy.

We've explored how to:

- Identify what you *really* want
- Recognize your negative thinking patterns
- Neutralize negative thoughts
- Take control with the **STOP & SWAP** method
- Create new and powerful thought habits
- Direct your thoughts to your goals repeatedly
- Be grateful and give daily thanks
- Use positive and empowering affirmations
- Say it loud and proud
- Write it down and commit to it
- Develop a relaxed state of mind
- Find the best times to practice positive thinking
- Avoid *can't* thinking or other negative language
- Remind yourself of all your positive qualities
- Be laser focused to turn your goals into a reality
- Find a happier, calmer and healthier you

However, it's important to understand that regardless of whether you develop a positive mindset, life will still throw up problems, challenges and times of hardship. Those who practice the art of positive thinking, and effectively use the techniques discussed in this book, will have a strong coping mechanism for such challenging times.

Remember, thoughts by themselves are only pieces of information (often wrong or exaggerated when it comes to negative thoughts). On their own they are not that powerful – it's the belief we give to them and the emotions they evoke in us that gives them power.

Make sure you focus at least some of your energies on positive thoughts each day, rather than unpleasant or self-destructive ones. Seek out reasons to be happy, motivated, grateful, focused and hopeful every day. Put your energies into achieving what you desire and helping others along the way.

"Give goodness to the day
and before you know it,
the day will be giving
goodness to you."
~ Terri Guillemets

Focus on what's possible – You may not be able to change things overnight, your goals may take time to become a reality and negative thoughts will creep in from time to time. However, knowing that you have empowering habits you can quickly call upon to can give you confidence to know that everything will be okay.

Use your power tools in the right way and you'll be amazed at the power you possess.

Understand and maximize these tools:

- The power of clearly stating what you want
- The power of being true to your values and purpose
- The power of positive affirmations
- The power of positive, proactive language
- The power of your imagination and visualizing
- The power of gratitude
- The power of positive writing
- The power of committing to a positive mindset
- The power of developing positive daily habits
- The power of believing in yourself
- The power of repetition

*"Keep your **thoughts** positive*
because your thoughts become your words.
*Keep your **words** positive*
because your words become your behavior.
*Keep your **behavior** positive*
because your behavior becomes your habits.
*Keep your **habits** positive*
because your habits become your values.
*Keep your **values** positive*
because your values become your destiny."
~ Mahatma Gandhi

To truly benefit from daily positive thinking take time to identify the methods and techniques that work for you. Incorporate them into your daily life, and explore how positive they make you feel.

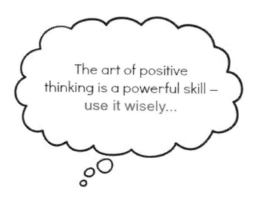

6

Next Steps

We really hope you've enjoyed reading the book, and found lots of inspiring ideas to get your creative and positive thoughts flowing!

To consistently achieve positive thoughts every day you now need to practice the techniques and methods we've discussed. We recommend the following to help you effortlessly build the habit of daily positivity:

Review the various steps outlined in Chapter 4, especially those detailed in the Subchapter 'Building Blocks For Effortless Daily Positivity'. Take time to review the processes outlined in the Subchapter on 'Laser Focus'. Focus on these steps alone, and master the relevant skills and you'll benefit by feeling more energized, determined, confident, brighter, healthier and ready to take on the world.

Read more on the subject of positivity. If you would like to explore more about the art of positive thinking then you may also enjoy the following titles by other authors:

Positivity: Top-notch Research Reveals the 3 to 1 Ratio That Will Change Your Life – Barbara Fredrickson

The Energy Bus: 10 Rules to Fuel Your Life, Work and Team with Positive Energy – Jon Gordon, Ken Blanchard

I Can Do It: How To Use Affirmations To Change Your Life – Louise L Hay

Positive Energy – 10 Extraordinary Prescriptions for Transforming Fatigue, Stress and Fear into Vibrance, Strength and Love – Judith Orloff

We also have other **FeelFabToday Guides** *available, which you may enjoy:*

  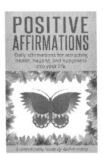

<u>www.feelfabtoday.com</u>

Practice, practice, practice. Take time every day to apply these powerful techniques, and to develop the skills that empower you to feel happy, calm and healthy.

Take Consistent and Meaningful Steps To Focus On Your Daily Positive Thoughts

*Pick out the methods that work
best for you.
Commit to being, doing and having
what you really want.*

Practice your positivity habits daily.

7

About The Author

Rachel Robins is the creator behind the feelfabtoday products. She has a passion for exploring and sharing ideas that centre on positivity & self improvement.

Rachel focuses her attention on how to help others feel as good as possible - using realistic feel-good techniques, healthy tips & a hefty dose of positivity. At the heart of the feelfabtoday products are methods on how to feel fabulous, look great, achieve more & live positively. These products are created with the help of a small team of talented people, who add their wisdom, knowledge and skills to the process, and who Rachel would like to thank for their continued efforts and support.

Rachel has worked in various senior management roles, where she's successfully practiced the art of conflict management, leadership, negotiation and change management.

Plus, she's trained many teams and individuals to achieve successful, target driven outcomes. Her range of interpersonal skills, life experience and self-help knowledge means she's able to share practical steps on how to take control of your life, develop a positive self image, and feel good about yourself.

She's put together this FeelFabToday Guide on *Positive Thoughts*, to help focus on overcoming negative thinking patterns, and to instead focus on a healthier, happier way of thinking. The Guide can be used as a source of inspiration and encouragement, to help create daily positive thoughts, and to turn each day into a great day.

Rachel's also written additional FeelFabToday Guides, designed to explore different areas of self empowerment, confidence building and feeling good about yourself. More information on these Guides can be found at www.feelfabtoday.com.

8

And Finally

**We really hope you found
this book helpful.**

We'd love it if you'd join us at:
twitter.com/feelfabtoday
www.feelfabtoday.com
We also welcome any comments or feedback,
so please feel free to get in touch with us:
hello@feelfabtoday.com

**Many thanks for reading our book. We wish you
every success in achieving your daily positivity...**